T0149403

INTUITION
WORKING TOOL

Sergio Antonio Meneghetti

authorHOUSE®

AuthorHouse™
1663 Liberty Drive
Bloomington, IN 47403
www.authorhouse.com
Phone: 1-800-839-8640

Published by AuthorHouse   10/06/2014

ISBN: 978-1-4969-3518-2 (sc)
ISBN: 978-1-4969-3517-5 (e)

Library of Congress Control Number: 2014914713

INTUITION
WORKING TOOL

I dedicate this book to:

GOD: Creator of all things
FAMILY: The source of my motivation and to all that
contributed and are still present in my Life
FRIENDS: that have inspired and helped
me to make this book a reality:

Pedro Mandelli
Robson Rodrigues

ACKNOWLEDGMENTS

This book would not have been possible without the added support and assistance of my friends:

Cover: Adelson Cavalcante
Editing; Elizabeth de Sa Castello Branco
Translation: Sonia Goncalves

CONTENTS

FOREWORD

The purpose of this work is to prove the existence of other sources of development that do not follow conventional methods. These types of development are sometimes known as intuition, inspiration or spirituality. These methods allow us to explore new horizons regarding evolution and science. The idea is to multiply the geniality that is within mankind paying attention to inner thoughts and listening to the heart: human beings will this way progress at a faster pace.

There are many in-depth studies made by accredited researchers, authors and scientists. These techniques are a constant presence in my life, a path that I follow as an apprentice to achieve my challenging objectives in life. I will also be discussing the subject in the professional field, as it is a powerful tool when applied wisely. My intent is to relay the message in a simple manner, so everyone will be benefited by the experience. As the author, I am the end user of this information and am gradually learning to work with these natural phenomena towards spiritual, moral and professional growth!

Preliminary considerations:

Few people are aware that in Brazil there is an interesting collection of works called the "New Civilization of the Third Millennium Herald", by Professor Pietro Ubaldi. His works are recognized for their instruction on developing high intuitive powers. My book seeks to summarize all the concepts presented on Professor Pietro Ubaldi's 24 volumes:

1. Great Messages (set of seven messages received through the intuition and life of the author).
2. Great Synthesis (summary and solutions of scientific and spiritual challenges through the intuitive process).

3. Nours (author's explanation about the techniques and reception of thought currents)

From the "Great Synthesis":

We all dream of finding a book that becomes a personal inspiration. Much like the dream house we find, a book can become a place in which we live in or come to live in. I realize that I have found my book called Great Synthesis by Pietro Ubaldi.

"We must read it! As I read it, I soar to higher spheres in awe!"

Monteiro Lobato, journalist and Brazilian author known by the simplicity of the messages in his books stated:
"The purpose of this book is not to undermine the science that has helped me so much in this quest, but only encourage the possibility that faith and science can work together."

Some famous people that used to exchange correspondence with Pietro Ubaldi:

Albert Einstein   Enrico Fermi   Ernest Bozzano

My words are just a mere spark when compared to the great Light of Ubaldi's work, but I will try to convey the truths that will allow us to follow a divine path. I am sure these insights will enrich and promote self-improvement to everyone.

Below are some sample questions that explore an almost unknown area. These questions are structured by a purely rational method. It disregards accepted paradigms, religions, and the lack of knowledge about the subject:

1. Up to which level what we think originates within ourselves or we experience the intuitive influence of the invisible plane?
2. Where do we get the inspiration source for the arts, like painting, poetry, literature to music?
3. What are the channels used by geniuses and prophets in their findings, their prophecies and their compositions?
4. How do we explain the extraordinary inspiration of apparently common people to produce the unconceivable?
5. What must be done in order to open such paths?

For us to obtain such answers we must be open to concepts of the mind and set aside dogmas and creeds. This opens the mind by releasing the knots of reason, and allows one to gather new knowledge so the pre-existent principles can evolve within mankind.

In the first instance we have to assimilate difficult concepts in our intellect, like the one concept of time and space, absolute or relative as they are considered to be part of whole, for they are after all related somehow.

Work also is based in moral principles. The qualifying selection, either in the workforce or on a personal level, we believe, in the future will be based on survival or necessity.

The employee of the future will have to excel not only in the workforce, but also to be above average as far as morals are concerned.

This standard will set corporations apart in the future. They will have to create ethical rules and conduct fair practices as the law of cause and effect will be present in all fields.

Society, like institutions or corporations, will learn to explore the best of each individual, not by imposing rules or programs, allowing them to be more confident on their own talents. When we do what we like and have aptitude for the task, the result is always better and greater. This attitude will promote less waste of personal energy or harm to the environment. It will bring happiness to all.

The emphasis today is based on personal characteristics, how to better interact and behave with colleagues, improving personal conduct. Mankind is in the process of being trained technically. What seemed to be a natural and personal process now is out in the open monitored externally by qualified professionals in human psychology.

The principle of how to perform allows space for how to be or to relate.

The external culture (e.g. degrees, specializations) is well established and accessible to all. Therefore, we have plenty of qualified professionals ready to fill all segments of the industry.

To be always ahead, the government, companies and institutions must always look for innovation. The self realization trails together along with inventions and productive processes. It is a new universe to be explored but old as life as we know it. . It is called moral evolution. It opens doors to a greater potential, much greater than we have known and witnessed so far. The keen awareness of our senses will play a key role in the moral intellectual, scientific and professional fields.

Intuition presents itself as a powerful tool to boost the progress of the areas above mentioned.

The professional will learn how to concentrate on his inner self, extracting better ideas and solutions when needed.

Properly used in the workforce, intuition can save time, money, avoid waste, prevent unwarranted expenses and will help to make wise decisions.

This tool can be used to point out the best direction to take when in doubt.

Regardless of the professional field, intuition is helpful to anyone because is the personal channel information, always updated because it is ahead of progress.

The intuition technique requires:

Evolution - the capacity to deal morally and culturally with new things
Renounce - incentive to spiritual progress that leads to happiness.
Kindness - promotes a sense of well being to all.
This is the best and most productive path that mankind can take.

"Anyone that wants to lead has the moral audacity for such".

Rarely our psychology can mix scientific concepts with spirituality
We cannot talk about intuition without mentioning the source of all: the Creator.

God is not limited to religion only, but also to all knowledge past, present and future.

Science is the result of our effort to understand His creation and how it works.

This mechanism can be understood by logic and reason, intuition, perception and wisdom.

The ignorance of the past associated with greed separated science from religion, but nowadays the paths have a tendency to merge because everything in the Universe is related.

We will compare intuition to a seed that will produce a tree.

None can "see" the characteristics of the tree from the seed, but it already has all the genetic information needed to be created.

Likewise, intuition also will bear its full potency someday but it will depend on evolution and science.

Intuition is the result of facts based on our experience, even though is hard to define it in depth. We cannot expect miracles, and we must isolate ourselves from the outside world: the key to understand this phenomenon is to experience it!

Science, to Science, Science exists!

While men lay over dead rocks, trying to find in old manuscripts the life mysteries by logic, new science brings messages, clearly, and fast through intuition.

The first is analytical and requires much knowledge, economic effort, personal, technological and time.
The second is synthetic and demands man's moral refinement, knowledge and personal effort.

The first requires analyses, interpretations and theories.
The second requires perception interpretations and learning.

The first studies the past.
The second throws man in the future.

The first is restricted to space and time.
The second is open to the Absolute.

The first is limited to reason.
The second has no limits.

The first is the core of all ancient values.
The second is the essential serum to bring life to the centuries that will come.

The first is a step gone.
The second is the platform that rises.

The first made men.
The second will make angels!

The first took you from ignorance of the mud from which you were created.

The second will show you heaven's mysteries from where you came.

The first chained you to principles.
The second will set you free by the will of God.

Science, creation of human labor, is the ladder that takes to the intimate knowledge of matter, lens allowing the search of the micro and macro universe, showing us a perfect and complex mechanism.

When science runs out of answers, the science that emanates from man's evolution will give answers through internal processes and will be able to explain all the phenomena as a whole rapidly through intuitive perception.

"Intuition is a science addressed to Science, because in it there is Science"

Sergio Antonio Meneghetti.

CHAPTER I

Definition of Intuition

Intuition: lat. Intueri

Capacity to perceive or discern in a clear and accurate way.
Capacity to foresee.
Contemplation by which one reaches real truth against the ones reached by reason or knowledge, discursive or analytical.
Connecting channels between the material and spiritual.

Everyone has intuition. Intuition is an inherent communication tool in a human being. Most of the time one cannot distinguish if it is a thought or external influence.

The manifestation is also identified with the famous instantaneous idea.

There are many ways to open the channels of intuition: meditation, prayer mind release etc. . . .

For each individual, there will be specific manifestations that are directly connected to his physical and spiritual evolution.The intuitive manifestations can have two origins: internal and external.

External Manifestation: influence of the invisible realm that motivates man to do good things and important warnings, as well as evil thoughts, which cause man, do bad things.

Internal Manifestation:
Internal manifestation comes in the shape of ideas.

It flashes in our mind and gives us a quick understanding about a subject or it shows us a new way of how to deal with a situation, enable us to visualize the mechanics of a work process or a situation that requires our participation directly or indirectly. Usually, this is one of the greatest clues that allows one to advance and progress.

On the internal manifestation, one can give direction when there is a planned objective and some training to deal with this type of intuitive reception. In this case, it is important to keep the mind free of rationalization, so the answers or solutions arrive at a practical and faster rate.

Through these two ways of manifestation people can be guided to find out which one is more his sensibility type.

We will make a comparison for better understanding:

The human mind is similar to an electronic reception apparatus: it will receive several signals or electromagnetic waves and will reproduce the signal effect from where it is synchronized. The programming will be good or bad according to the transmitting source. We will have good intuition if we are connected to a good station. If we have bad reception we will have a destructive intuition. Usually if the mind is not in sync adequately, or ignores it, only static will be heard.

Nowadays, science has advanced in brain studies and it can determine the areas where the phenomenon and its effects happen,

It makes the connection between the brain and electronic equipments and begins to understand in detail the human" hardware".

Physical and spiritual health balance, are very important, to receive good intuition and they must be in harmony.

So far we have discussed the hardware or brain, but how is the software connected in this complex and perfect machine?

Let's assume by comparison that the body is the hardware and to complete the machine, the spirit, soul or essence is the software.

A computer without energy, even being the best, will not produce any results. It needs energy to activate the software.

The human body is similar, because without the vital energy, it is just an agglomerate of molecules. What makes things "happen' is the sum of "me essence" which is the software coupled to the body that is the hardware.

The self is the commander of the body, the brain by itself does not create anything. The perfect association spirit and matter creates the thoughts that will be the basis of evolution.

Have you noticed that when an individual dies, or the vital energy leaves the body, the cells, molecules and atoms disconnect from each other, and the process of desegregation start?

Another interesting factor in studies made with terminally ill patients, at the time of death is that there is a body weight loss of around twenty grams.

Could it be the vital energy mass or spirit? Probably!

Another interesting example: many people have already witnessed or knew a person who claims seeing somebody that is already dead. In some cases the spirit gives advice or asks for help.

A famous example of this phenomenon is The Virgin in Fatima in Portugal. She appeared to three children. These spirits or saints do not have a material brain like us, however they talk, see teach, move, etc. . . .

So we can conclude that the brain is a receptive machine of something that does not belong to matter and this same machine works according to its condition, i. e. perfectly or with restrictions. The conclusions from these facts show that:

The healthy human machine is very important to support the spirit: a defective hardware will not make the software function properly.

The brain has in its structure specific areas for each function therefore it has the area from which intuition is received.

Higher morals are the tuner for a positive reception.

Since the beginning of time, humans have worked with this tool called intuition, even though the great majority was not aware of its existence.

Many advances in science, art in general, discoveries, or mere warnings were made based on this phenomenon.

Man has an unbelievable potential to be explored. The current stages of development, technological and cultural can be used to examine carefully the being's inner faculties.

He has to be aware that he must utilize this tool wisely for noble purposes only.

A good person uses the knife to prepare food in the kitchen. An evil person uses it to hurt someone. We are entering the Third Millennium.

According to several spiritual and philosophical sources this is the "Mental Era".

The human mind, more advanced will bring more sustainable and economical improvements regarding the Earth's resources.

We are not setting reason aside; after all it plays an important role in the human context. It is through reason that there is understanding to be used on a daily basis.

Intuition

Intuition, means of communication
Internal sensor of happiness and love
Taking from the moral space
The Creator's invisible life.

The one that feels deep inside
And prepares to receive
The profound knowledge
To better the world.

Timeless treasure
That comes to us
Only with dedication
And also with sacrifice.

We are chosen
When we deserve it
When in our heart
We receive knowledge.

Beautiful words
At times naive
Are in the weavings
Of our Lord.

CHAPTER II

Company's Objective

Let's make a detailed analysis of the role an enterprise plays in a person's life:

Usually an enterprise starts out small; its main purpose is to support the founder financially, through his capacity, work, and persistence. In many cases the company will grow very powerful, known and respected worldwide.

So far, we have observed the company's growth through the eyes of the founder.

Let's observe through the employee's perspective: the owner plays an important role in company's growth and also profits from it. His survival as well as his family is guaranteed.

But is the true purpose of the company, to focus only on the employee's survival and the owner's prosperity?

Of course not! When this relationship occurs, it includes the progress and maturing of both sides, advances in the technological field, communication, health, information, Men evolve through work, which demands improvement, compels him to search for more daring and creative enterprises: the backdrop will be the financial gain and business survival. But if we analyze through a higher level and put aside the financial aspect, we will find that the social mechanism enables the planet to advance! That is the true purpose of corporations, to promote a dignified advance for mankind.

It is at work that people interact, socialize and grow as individuals.

As a rule, a person spends more time at work than at home; therefore we can conclude that corporations have a noble purpose before God.

It is a gatherer of ideas and ideals; it is a testing field for the human capacity. It is a molding environment.

If we take an X-ray of companies, large corporations are concerned about a high academic profile of their employees, the selections is strict, with resumes, group seminars, interviews even using television to hire prospective employees.

There are a great number of employees desperately trying to improve their skills to prevent them from losing their job. It is very stressful. Only time will reveal the consequences that this condition causes and hard to predict what type of return companies will get from it.

The employee and company should not depend solely on the manager for performance and internal growth. Employees have to be stimulated; there has to be balance of responsibilities facilitating advanced scientific, cultural and financial wealth.

Corporations are also receptive to the use of intuition and spirituality in the workplace.

That was what motivated me to write this book, by giving testimony to full experiences with personal and practical knowledge, not only providing a large amplitude of definitions and conjectures but how this intuitive potential will be effective.

We do not want to be critical of any related matter because we do believe that:

"To criticize is easier than to make a mistake". Each individual shares what has learned which is very valuable."

When something is crucial to the world's advancement, it becomes important to many people in many aspects.

Let's analyze what the large companies have in common:

They equip themselves with administrative packages to maintain their management updated and competitive, with strategic plans, logistics and, production controls. They also invest in personnel, heavy in high technology and care for the environment.

Who will survive in the future, since all companies are equipped with the best the marketplace has to offer?

What will make a difference if all have access to the best qualified employees?

Why companies fail even though they have all these advantages?

Could it be that the competition is stagnant in management techniques?

Survival, differential, continuity, and the new will be ingrained in human talent, not only in their academic degree, but also in what they have to offer in their moral and perceptive abilities and the wisdom to apply these talents.

The combination of intuition, spirituality, and knowledge will play a major role in the competition. These factors will strengthen people being better at work and generating optimum results. It is like creating one unique body, for a specific goal!

Even though the world is going through some difficulties, the tendency of the globalized world is to unite in order to survive.

Thus, society has to become unique, sharing a balanced purpose for the benefit of all.

Uno

From globular energy to holiness, the soul tries its first steps, dives into eternity, and fights for survival, creates to evolve from a basic and primitive being to the perfect self where there are no more flesh limitations and painful hard lives. We are all connected; we are divine cells and independent. We are eternal, part of the Divine; we are Divine because we came from the Creator.

We are love expressed in life form, the most beautiful truth that the human being can understand; we are eternal cells of the Divine. We must then, love one another as brothers.

The "self" will only feel complete when it becomes part of the universe. Today, the mind is the most and more advanced legacy we own, it has to open the doors for better understanding, perfection and help for those that follow their own path.

"There is only one purpose and the integration is the great conquest we can achieve, because it will be the biggest enlightenment of qualities that we will build inside ourselves".

Sergio Meneghetti

This conquest will not be rapid to obtain, but the sooner we start the process of development, the better and faster the results will come.

The first obstacle will be to understand this reality: experts in human relations that have the purpose of bringing to fruition the necessary tools will have the most difficult task in identifying people that are ready for such endeavor.

There is always the first step, like in all fields of evolution. The inertia will be broken and the wheel of progress will be responsible for the maturity of a new psychology process in the workplace.

We extracted a text from the Internet, which will clarify what we are trying to transmit to our readers.

We take the opportunity to congratulate the Brazilian author that describes accurately his contribution to the betterment of Brazil.

Text written by a Brazilian who lives in Europe posted in the Internet:

I have been an employee of Volvo, a Swedish corporation for 18 years.

To work with them is very interesting. Any project here takes 3 years to materialize, even when the idea is simple and genial. It is a rule! The Brazilians, Americans, Asians get anxious for immediate results. But our sense of urgency does not produce any result within this time frame.

The Swedish, have endless meetings and work at a slower pace. At the end, the results coincide with the advancement of technology and according to necessity. Very little is wasted there!

- The country is the size of Sao Paulo, Brazil.
- The country has 2 million citizens.
- Their biggest city Stockholm has 500 thousand people.

- Their multinational corporations: Volvo, Scandia, Erickson, Nokia, Nobel Biocare, etc.....
- Volvo manufacturers the rocket engines for NASA.

The Swedish, may be wrong, however they are the ones who pay our salaries. Collective culture I am not aware of a country that has a better global culture than the Swedes.

Below an example of this conclusion:

I arrived there in 1990. A colleague picked me up at the hotel every morning

We would arrive early at Volvo and he would park far away from the entrance. The weather was snowy and icy cold in September. The parking lot has capability for 2000 automobiles. After getting to know him a little better, one morning I asked him if he had his assigned place to park, but he replied that the reason he did that was because he took in consideration that fact that late people needed to be closer to the entrance and the early ones had time to walk! I was amazed at the reply and did reconsider my values!

Another article seen in the Internet:

There is a big movement in Europe today, called Slow Food. Slow Food International with the snail as their logo has its headquarters in Italy. Their concept is that we must eat and drink slowly, savoring the food and enjoying the preparation, amid family and friends.

The idea is to counteract the Fast Food concept as a lifestyle, which the Americans turned into a culture.

The interesting thing is that this movement is serving as a basis for a bigger concept called Slow Europe as documented in the Magazine "Business Week", in a European article.

The basis for everything is anchored on haste, the craziness generated by globalization: quantity against quality.

As per Business Week article, the French workers, even though they work fewer hours (35 per week) are much more productive than the Americans and English. The Germans who implanted the 28. 8hours a week in their workforce witnessed their productivity to increase 20%.

This so called slow attitude is drawing the attention of the Americans, worshippers of the Fast and the Do it now. So this approach does not mean do less or be less productive.

It means do things with more quality, productivity, with more accuracy and attention to detail with less "stress".

It means enjoying family, friends, leisure, small communities, concentrating in the "local" present against the "global": indefinite and impersonal. It means the retake of the basic human needs, the small pleasures, simplicity of daily life and even interaction between religion and faith.

It means a work environment less stressful, more enjoyable, "lighter", thus more productive, where happy people, do what they do best, with pleasure.

Could it be that the old sayings: "Slowly but surely"! "Haste makes waste"! again deserves our consideration on these hard times?

Would it be better if our corporations came up with serious programs with quality without haste to increase productivity and services without losing the quality of self?

In the movie "Scent of a Woman" there is an unforgettable scene, in which a blind man portrayed by Al Pacino, asks a lady to dance and she tells him that she cannot dance because her fiancé will arrive at any moment.

"But in one moment one lives a lifetime!" and then leads her to dance Tango. It is the best scene of the movie.

Some people race against time, but only are successful in suffering heart attacks. For others, time lingers: they become apprehensive with the future and forget to live the present.

Everyone has time at his disposition, 24 hours a day.

The difference is the quality of time spent. We need to learn how to take advantage of every moment, because as John Lennon put it:

"Life is what happens while you are making plans!"

Congratulations for reading till the end! Many will not read this message, because they cannot waste their time in this globalized world. Think and ponder. Is it worth it not to spend time with family, a loved one, to go fishing on weekends?

It could be too late! Know how to learn in order to survive!!!!

Something interesting in the context was the Being quality, for there is such a big worry in "having" that people will do anything to get it and end up frustrated in the future, They look back and realize how long they neglected the people that matter. Actually the inner existence will be the only true factor worth taking to eternity.

The big names in History did not became famous by what they owned, but by what they were.

"Personal value is not bought, is earned!"

Sergio A. Meneghetti

To have or to be!

When we open our eyes for the first time, we only have ourselves, because we do not have yet the power to have.

When our eyes close for the last time, we know that we have nothing but ourselves, then we realize that we do not have what we think we do!

We are born and leave life with the illusion that we own something and that the more we own, the more we are: we only wake up when the illusion of having ends with the loss of things that seem endless.

We own nothing in this school called Life, however not owning does not lessen the person, just the opposite, the higher the conscience, the better it will be!

Man has to be above the "want to have": it can only be attained when self "lives" and to live is not the same as to exist.

To live is to recognize what life has to offer: happiness, sorrow, rest, tiredness, love and suffering, the foe and the friend, riches and poverty, life or death.

Do not let life lead you; you must take control!

Only life is truly yours, the biggest gift from God, then the most important factor is to be!

Do not stand in the shadow of Life, resting or waiting for things to happen, be the light of your Life, living intensely every moment with love and courage.

Your existence can be guided by two factors: knowledge acquired in the life struggle and pure friendship of people that were with you while you were living!

The most important truth is:
Live to be, not to have!

Sergio Meneghetti

CHAPTER III

Work

What is the essence of work?

Human being's energy spent outside idleness is defined as work.

In physics it is defined as: work is force times distance or displacement.

But going deeper, we find that work is material result started from the immaterial, desire or will, or better defined as the extension of conscience.

Conscience that can be called I., the one that commands the matter in body form. Following this trend of thought, we command our actions, even though we are not aware of it.

The reader may ask what these concepts have to do with our daily work?

It is simple: if God created things according to His will, naturally the concept is the same, for we also do things out of our will. Therefore, work is an action of divine nature; the invisible is modeled in matter. If work is a constant activity, then we can assume that God never stops working.

Work is not limited only to the "daily bread", but in all activities: art is the result of the artist's creation, sport, the result of the athlete's activity; knowledge and thought transmitted through voice are "work."

Men should not only work for survival, he has to perceive it as an extension of himself.

Work is the reflex of materialized life. Work well done pleases the worker and God; all work directed towards progress is like a small block in the construction of the majestic building called evolution.

Which type of work will be the most important?

All work done with love is important, does not rely on positions or outcome; all play an important role in the overall picture.

Any construction, no matter how extensive has to have a group participation: we can appreciate the outside beauty of a great building; however the foundation, deep into the ground is the one that gives support to the structure.

From the humblest worker, to the most important, both equally have the same value before the Creator.

That is a good reason for having mutual respect, leaving aside pride and vanity.

Because everything in the Universe needs balance, work also has to be viewed the same way: work is our responsibility, but it also has to be balanced with other activities: family life, leisure, arts, socializing, etc.

When men are obsessed in obtaining material gain, he is denigrating the true meaning of work, causing unbalance.

This unbalance will manifest in the form of stress, relationship problems, chronic diseases, ruin on family life when men overdo it, and sometimes it can be fatal.

It does not matter the function we have at hand, doing the best will separate amateurs from professionals, it is our passport to something higher, even if is not where we are today.

Every person who strives to transmit the acquired knowledge to others who come their way, is self-assured, wise and above all, responsible.

Another very important factor is that work should the motivation for Construction and not a vital energy spent with destructive intentions.

What is transcribed here is already common knowledge for empowered professionals and those that have the noble mission of relaying information to the worker.

There are many professionals, instructing a new generation of professionals through seminars, courses, literary works and other means of communication.

Below some advice to the young starting in the marketplace:

- Be yourself, be humble, listen more than talk, show respect to the people around you, accomplish your goals through a job well done, and forget politics, for it can get you into compromising situations.

- Never underestimate anyone, appearances are deceiving, we always have something to learn.
- Today you will start as hardware, but time and wisdom will turn you into software.
- Through your journey, you will commit many mistakes, be responsible and learn from them. Every situation has a positive side, usually are the lessons we must learn.
- When at the top and pride takes control of you do not look up, because you might fall into a hole that will awaken you from this illusion.
- Do not misuse people that cross your path, make true friends out of them and they will give you the moral support when you need it.
- Never stop learning, life never stands still, also do not try to control everything; you are the most important person in this context. It is not very important to have an overload of information, but know how to use the ones at hand, it is wise not to get lost in it but to know how to find it rapidly because today we have all the tools available.
- If in a race to get in a higher position the probability of success is 50%, this part depends on you; the other half is product of circumstances. If you fail, still be the best in what you do.
- If your objective is only material, you will probably be successful, but in the future the pocket will be full, but the heart will be empty. The reason is because you were not yourself.
- Be grateful for the opportunities of work: people ask, plead, make promises to get a job, but sooner they feel bored, lazy, wait anxiously for the weekend, not for the leisure, but to avoid working and get sad when Sunday night comes, for they will have to go to work on Monday. They will appreciate work only when they lose it.
- To do what we like and try to be the best at it with dedication will bring happiness; money will be a consequence, not a reason.

- In the future your children will admire you for what you are and not for what you have.
- Material gains are important, though. If people did not prosper in this area, we all would be without a job today. Wisdom must be exercised and balance is the key.
- The greatest reward of work is the result, it is the trophy, the productive energy materialized, and it is her role in the order of the Universe.
- If you ever feel that you suffered injustice, you will have two options: bow your head and mope about it or stand up and fight to be vindicated.

We all have highs on our professional careers; the secret is to know how to manage these phases wisely, because when you reach low, you will feel either satisfaction for a job well done or remorse for the negligence. . .

At work as well as at home we will have to interact with people with distinct personalities, this interaction is very important to our personal growth.

Just like at home, work people, must be respected by their moral conduct and not as a result of circumstance. We must bear in mind that power is constructive when we know how to use it. However the opposite is true if this power is not beneficial to all concerned.

The highest recognition for a professional is his work: his soul and dignity are more valuable than money or a short-lived hierarchy.

The worker

The worker does not tire
Works endlessly
If there is work, he does not rest
Work is his life.

His hands mold the Earth
Builds with real bricks, the world
Creates opportunity, that does not end
Is deep in his endeavor.

Builder of humanity
Brings the example in passion
Works in the infamy's bed
Reaching our heart.

His work is example
His attitude is noble
His work builds the temple
His construction is pure beauty.

Building with love
The temple of salvation
Soothing our pain
And showing us evolution.

Sergio A. Meneghetti

CHAPTER IV

Virtues and Vices

When we come up with an idea, personal, professional or cultural, at first we feel it is the best idea, considering the circumstances, but everything changes constantly and something new replaces the original thought. That is called evolution.

There is constant change and same principle applies to mankind physically, culturally and spiritually.

All starts from the imperfect towards the perfect and that is why it is common to find people with different levels of understanding and trends of thought.

Life was, is, and will be originated from the same source (GOD), but in distinct and individual moments. Nothing in the Universe is the same.

Flaws:-Through times we find that certain behaviors or attitudes which were accepted in the past might not be accepted today, and some habits or customs presently can be interpreted as a personal flaw in the future. Today, human imperfections are associated to personal ignorance: conscious or unconscious.

The conscious flaw is a personal option, the individual does not want or have the courage to improve, and is oblivious to the world's evolution.

The unconscious flaw - when an individual is not aware of his attitudes or accepts them as normal: in reality he will be better prepared to awaken to reality, for he is not prepared to answer with negatives.

In corporations, like in a social environment, we will find a variety of people that are within the same parameters culturally; however their moral principles will vary.

What productive results will this group have?

If only mechanical functions are required and there is no interaction among people, the work performance will produce a satisfactory standard of quality.

However, when worker's communication between departments is necessary to resolve an issue, the company will not be productive if the best interest of the company is not the main focus.

Selfishness and conflicting interests still are ingrained in human nature.

These flaws are detrimental to a company, sometimes even causing it to bankrupt.

A company is similar to a body, where the members are the material organization and the mind is the workforce.

As the body chemistry functions in ideal synchronism for the well being of the body, so is the workforce within the company, the professionals have to operate in a similar fashion in a healthy company and vice versa.

Most people have heard that: People make the Company! Sometimes the manager distances himself from his subordinates, and employees see the superior as an enemy, someone that exploits them for his own benefit, even though both are employees working towards a common goal.

The Supervisor and the employee run the same risk of getting fired, being transferred to another branch, getting a promotion, etc. . . .

The above is a typical example that wastes energy causing losses to all concerned.

After all:

If the Company is OK, I am OK. The Company is not OK; it can mean the end for me!"

Human beings are imperfect. There is a big necessity to get rid of this "heavy armor"; one must be lapidated like a diamond to reveal his inner brilliance. A job is an excellent "laboratory" for this transformation.

Virtues:

Virtues are acquired through a long journey, it cannot be obtained in just one lifetime, it takes learning, losses, victories, trial and error a constant struggle, between good and evil.

If we take the time to know ourselves and recognize our faults and shortcomings, we will win the battle. By ignoring the mechanics of life we have a tendency to believe that we are always right, but this is an illusion! That stunts our advancement as human beings and delays vital knowledge.

We must live each day to the fullest, nothing stay the same. When things seem to be stagnant, actually we are the ones "frozen in time": we are unable to observe the eternal advancement.

The world travels within the Universe very rapidly, and we are involved in this evolution at the same speed, in each fraction of second everything is changing, therefore we also must change.

All transformation has to be positive and progressive.

Just because we do not believe in something that does not mean that it does not exist, and if it does our disbelief does not erase the fact that people are capable of absorbing details which will be given later.

The path is progressive, and will refine our actions and thoughts, transforming them in virtues. The raw material lies on; love, detachment, self-denial, work, faith, knowledge and charity.

The positive results in the workplace happen only when the employees are in harmony, work becomes pleasure, there is great productivity and business prosper.

The virtuous person depends on his work for support, makes mistakes, but learns from them. He respects the hierarchy from the lowest to the highest job title, helps people indistinctively, enhances the qualities of others and discreetly coaxes proud people to "see" the light.

His words inspire, without criticizing, try to understand people's faults, because he also makes mistakes, shares his main goal as it is everybody's goal: to win the everyday struggle together.

It may seem far reached utopia, but we can be assured that this is the natural way for things to happen: people that are in the workplace for a long time will confirm the process.

The moral values gain a new significance as opposed to the past where intellectual capacity was more important.

With the technology advancement, virtue will be measured by equipment. There is a photographic process called Kirlean that measures the magnetic field irradiated by a person. It detects the disposition of a person at that moment; in the future it will be able to detect moral values.

As an example: a healthy person physically and spiritually will irradiate a bright light, a sick person will irradiate a dim and hazy light.

With this information, there is no secret formula, only analyses of facts, mathematically.

Wisely speaking, job opportunities are available for virtuous individuals and doors are closing to the ones that are not.

Virtue

What is done is done
Ignore the undone
This will only resolve
When in virtue, it will be perfect!

Sergio A. Meneghetti

CHAPTER V

Spirituality

As the old adage goes: Football and religion cannot be argued about!

Which is the best religion?

It is the one where we feel we belong, where we experience peace; to summarize it all denominations are good and one must respect the diversity of beliefs without prejudice.

Every religion is beneficial in direct proportion to the believer.

Religion makes us transcend the purpose of our existence, we look forward to eternity.

We have the moral responsibility to develop our spirituality and make it an extension of our daily living.

God does not discriminate people by religion, but He knows our hearts, for what we are, not by what we have or think we are.

Mankind still create obstacles in this matter, however all messages from above preach brotherhood. We must change our inner selves to understand that we are part of a whole and that our well being depends on others.

Irony
While love connects us
Religion separates us!

This is my point of view and no one is obligated to accept what is stated in this book. I have a lot to learn and do not "own the truth".

What is the relationship between work, company and spirituality?

Like in church, it is through reaching a higher spiritual level that man feels "light", the mind opens up and the environment is in harmony!

If we apply this to the workplace, things improve; great results will happen for the employee as well for the company.

The connection with God does not have to be only at the church or at home, it should also be extended to the working place, to leisure, when away on a trip, etc

It should be part of our daily routine to ask for protection and insight.

When we are confronted with difficulties, it is best to retire to a quite place, reflect about the situation and ask God for guidance. Surely we will improve the chances of making the right decisions when we recover our equilibrium, with a relaxed mind.

This practice should be put into use, only when is necessary. We do not want to transform the workplace into a church!

Performance at work will improve, accidents will be avoided, harmony will reign when people are contented at work, their life also improves because they will bring home good energy after a day's work. It is very important to have a connection between material and spiritual, we all profit from it and peace is achieved. Who does not want a better place to live?

Usually one third of life is spent at work and this period of time carries a lot of weigh on the remaining hours of the day!

Time

It was about time
That I began to understand time
Yesterday I had no time
Today I make time.

Do not waste time
Do not delay on time
Value your time
While there is time.

We have all the time
When we spend quality time
Leaving our mark in time
When we are fair all the time.

In time
I speak to you of time
Now that I have the time
Love you history, love your time!

Sergio A. Meneghetti

CHAPTER VI

Management Systems

When managing a corporation, regardless of the size, the executive in command has to be prepared to keep up with innovation.

He also has an enormous responsibility in his hands. His decisions influence the success of the company, and the fate of hundreds of people. That is his greatest personal challenge before the Creator. He has the responsibility to stimulate progress in mankind.

There is a mechanism in our lives constituted of several factors, each with its own functions to ensure adequate performance. Each person has to do his part to keep up with the necessary changes to maintain the great wheel moving. The professional evolution must be permanent because if there is role exchange, it will create room for another professional to grow.

The dynamics of work is comparable to life; whoever is not working is not living.

Each organization has its own characteristics, and for each there will be a specific management system.

A system can work very well for a company and not be adequate for another; it is up to management to identify the right system that attends the needs of the organization.

Great personalities and experts usually dictate the rules on how to better manage a company. This is normal procedure in the corporative world. However, even with strategic plans apparently foolproof, they do not prevent difficult situations to happen in business. The reason being that nobody can predict or control the future. It is impossible to control clients, suppliers as well as the climate and world's economical ups and downs.

The beauty of management lies on the humility to follow new alternatives, when necessary, by listening and always learning: hierarchy doesn't make anybody infallible. The manager does not have a crystal ball, but intuition can help to detect, by internal process, the best way to conduct the "corporate vessel".

Solidary Management

Hardly there is a position that does not need external support. That is able to execute the job independently. Then solidarity between colleagues becomes a priority to ensure that the work is harmonic and progressive.

To spread this solidarity practice, will be very beneficial to the end result.

When there is solidarity among workers, thankfulness and recognition will be present: adding these attributes will start a chain reaction.

If there is guidance, will, and predisposition, the effect will spread beyond the workers in question, reaching other sectors and can become a role model for the company as a whole. . .

Can you imagine a solidary work environment among people and how much synergy could be created?

Solidarity in personal life is realization, power, growth, and recognized as an act of greatness.

Life happens in a universal context and all is somehow connected. There is a tendency of separating things trying to ignore the fact that any mechanism that works in personal or social life, will also work in the professional and religious realm.

If moral acts are used for recognition and as example, why not apply them into the workplace? The results will be positive and all concerned will benefit from it.

A team, where its members are united and solidary always will be ahead of others. That is the secret.

When there is competition that attracts selfishness and separation; everybody will lose, starting from the most important characteristic: moral!

It is interesting to observe, when there are openings for promotion in companies, the great majority of workers instead of promoting their abilities for the job, prefer to point out other's mistakes, to slander their image before their superiors. It is disappointing!

It is the old politics of save yourself, if you can.

That is when the masks fall and show the true colors of each person. By the same token, whoever is ethical has nothing to worry about because in any situation he is himself.

The message this book tries to relay to readers is information so balance can be achieved among professionals, so the human potential in the company is more productive.

The best tools in the workforce if not used correctly will be a waste of time and will delay profits, so important to the business.

Management that utilizes wisdom and common sense will guarantee more satisfactory results than the more academic theories but with less impact in the group's mentality, or will to accept ideas.

To insure harmony between workers and managers, a commitment towards mutual respect has to exist in order to bind them to a common goal.

Delegating orders and then demanding results, is a thing of the past. Working in harmony ensures results well above 90% as opposed to 60-80% in the old system.

What is the key element to achieving a common denominator between superiors and employees? It is a consciousness which includes maturity, wisdom and love: an understanding that generates unity and remains strong and secure. When we are optimistic, the universe conspires in our favor and all obstacles are overcome.

Work will have a new meaning, and will not be boring or merely a "services rendered" endeavor, it will be joyous goal to be achieved.

To manage a group and obtain good results, the most important factor is the mutual respect between the manager and the employees.

The manager has to motivate his group by being humble and having knowledge. Arrogance will insure obedience, but not progress or prosperity.

The employee, who constitutes the majority, has to look up to his boss as someone that supports the team by considering their needs. This help and commitment guarantee results where everyone benefits.

Position cannot be synonymous with power. A healthy hierarchy is made of basic steps that enable a human being to grow emotionally and materially.

Without a considerate commander, there are no subjects.

By pointing out the ideal scenario for good management, we will have a favorable environment that will thrive with Intuition. The manager and his group will be aware of their responsibilities as a whole and the entire organization will work in harmony.

It requires practice and awareness. Not everyone will be in the same consciousness level and should not try to be detrimental to the people concerned: everyone will contribute accordingly to their abilities.

The secret lies in being prepared, to be able to identify the information, work it out, and provide a function that is positive and productive.

The great benefit of intuition is to acquire the knowledge in an unconventional way which saves time through the phases of production.

It minimizes effort and opens doors that are vital to reaching new objectives.

Intuition can be used and be helpful in all corporate levels and has nothing to do with the employee's educational background.

It will facilitate the performance of any strategic plan a company may choose.

Imagine how much revenue music generates in this world?

It is fabulous; few realize that the raw material for most part is from intuitive origin.

The most beautiful musical compositions come from the effort to produce beauty in harmony with all the elements concerned. This phenomenon also occurs in other aspects of art. Therefore, intuition happens when we work in harmony with one another and a perfect composition is created. It generates a great revenue potential in the company as well as in the quality of life and the environment.

When one saves steps in the corporate process, one also avoids waste and causes productive improvements to happen.

To manage is not only knowing how to, is also being able to perceive quickly and clearly the modifications to be made and take decisions most accurately possible.

The command of a corporation, government, institution has to have the nobility to be the conductor par excellence.

The Conductor

What a timeless beauty
In his face, tenderness
Life conducted by Him
Is pure candor.

His prayer tames the Earth
It is happy with kindness
Eases the war pains
And teaches charity.

It is excellence in love
It is a friend and protector
It is great in humanity
It is our Conductor.

His life was an example
Gave Life with eagerness
Was elected King
In a land of love and pain.

Enlightens the conscience
In reason and science
It is the shortest path.
It is the synthesis in essence.

It elevates us in humility
Does not matter the evil
What receives is Love
From the meek and the Creator

CHAPTER VII

Attitude

The Earth has about 7 billion inhabitants and is going through an accelerated transformation in all fields.

Our planet became global; the information is almost instantaneous, on the four corners. There are religious movements, for the peace, war, equality rights, racism, freedom, etc. . . .

It is a frantic race for power and possessions, for status, fame, conquest, comfort or simply to survive.

There is so much happening around us that we do not have the opportunity to find out where we are headed.

What is the address where one wants to get to?

What is to be expected in the meantime?

For everything that one struggles for, is mankind aware of the result generated at this moment?

Is the worry only personal and now, leaving the problems to the heirs?

Are the actions creative or just extractive?

How the concepts and values will be seen?

To advance or feel secure on what took so long to achieve?

If man could come back in fifty years, to start over how would he like to find this world?

When a man is close to death, how would his family evaluate his life?

Someone that conquered everything, but lost his dignity and character or obtained enough but honorably?

Surely, in the math of life, adding the actions, is the result going to be positive or negative?

There are many questions and probably few stop to ponder this topic called existence.

To exist is at least interesting: I am here, see, hear, observe, understand, participate, think, realize, search, love, suffer, hate, cry, miss somebody, happiness, sadness, fear, courage,

I am a father, I am a son, perceive what is coming and what is not.

I have feelings, passions, I am a believer, a non-believer, look forward to tomorrow even though I'm not sure it will happen, I live only my today, and it does not belong to me anymore, so it is very complex.

If to be alive is so complex there must be a reason beyond trivialities that gets so much validation?

What is required so evolution can happen?

This spring activator is called positive attitude: is the action charged with courage and energy and it is the action that only the daring can take.

It is the struggle of those who defy the unknown and sacrifice themselves for the common good. That is the compassionate man, a persistent genius, is the guiding sage, the mystic!

Explaining is the pure teaching in gestures.

It is about ordinary individuals doing the extraordinary!

To them we are forever grateful for all their advances and worldly wisdom.

To be a capable person, a good number of questions above will have to be answered, because these answers and the conscious work will carve this profile as a person and as a professional.

In the professional realm, we have to choose: either to be a mediocre worker or the one that goes the extra mile.

The professionals with a better chance of survival will be the ones that have a life goal based on wisdom and positive attitudes, capable of promoting the dynamic differential that business demands.

There are no shortcuts in the evolution and moral process: no magic techniques will transform people overnight into better citizens. It will be patient and conscious training and the sooner starts, the better!

Below some examples of attitude:

Citing the 2004 Olympic Games that were held in Athens, Greece, few remember who won the marathon, but all remember the athlete that won third place, after being pushed out of the race by a crazy spectator. The noble attitude of Vanderlei Cordeiro forgiving the culprit that cost him his victory touched the world. A true champion for sure. It emphasized where the true value lies: this noble attitude placed the runner above the winner.

Another example is Mahatma Gandhi, who by persistence, courage, detachment and without violence was able to obtain India's independence from the English. .
A world example of outstanding moral transcendence!

Francisco Candido Xavier dedicated his life to charity, being a live antenna between heaven and earth, bringing solace and important information to people.
He wrote more than 400 books never profited from it surviving only from the fruits of his labor as a public employee.

Martin Luther King-, a protestant american pastor, political activist Americano, became one of the most important leaders of black civil rights in the United States and the world.
Noble attitudes like these mentioned above attest the character of a true man!

Persistence
(extracted from internet)

A man invests all he has in a small office. He works non-stop and sleeps there. To keep afloat, he uses his wife's jewelry as collateral.

When he presents his finished product, the large corporation does not accept it, claiming it is below their standards of quality.

He goes back to school for another two years. His colleagues and teachers would mock him, calling him a dreamer.

Finally the company that had rejected him accepts his project after two years.

During the war his factory is bombarded twice and almost destroys everything.

He rebuilds the factory, but then an earthquake wipes out his business.

When war is over, there is a gasoline shortage and he cannot use his car to buy food for his family. He attaches a small motor to his bike and rides the streets.

The neighbors love the invention and soon he runs out of motors.

He decides to build a factory to market his latest invention, but cannot afford it. He decides to look for investors. Asks for financial backing from 15000 stores spread out around the country.

Since it was a great idea; he finally got the funding needed from 5000 stores to build his factory.

This is the saga of Soichiro Honda founder of Honda Corporation one of the most powerful and respected automotive industries in the world. He did not allow the obstacles to prevent him from reaching his goals.

A true example of persistence and inspiration to all.

If you are used to complaining, it's time to stop! What we know is a drop of water! What we do not know is the size of an ocean.

Remember: our day does not end at dusk and always starts again next day, do not despair, and let's wake up every day like we were discovering a new world.

And most important, let's not forget GOD!

Personally, for the first nine years I tried to be hired by my Company and I was employed for 27 years. It was worth it! The company was excellent!

There are many more great people who dedicated their lives towards a better world, some lost their lives.

On a popular Brazilian television show "Fantastico", the newswoman Gloria Maria was reporting on a trip Paulo Coelho (famous Brazilian writer) made to Russia.

During the trip, she interviewed an eighty year old lady that knitted wool booties and sold them, giving the proceeds to charity institutions.

A wonderful example of good will and action overcoming age and convenience.

When one takes action with energy, anything can happen!

Another example extracted from the Internet

A men looking for a job goes to Microsoft Corp and asks for a position as a plumber. He is interviewed and is asked to test a very sophisticated plunger.

He passes the test and is instructed to give his e-mail so he can fill out the application and receive the work schedule for the next day. He does not own a computer

He cannot be hired because he does not have an e-mail address.

With only US12. 00 in his pocket, desperate, he goes to the market and buys 10 kilos of strawberries.

He sells the strawberries going door to door and in less than 2 hours, duplicates his investment. He repeats the operation three more times and returns home with US $ 60. 00.

He realized that he could survive by selling fruit. Soon he was able to afford a truck and today he is one of the biggest food distributors in the USA.

Five years later he decided to buy life insurance for his family and contacted an agent to discuss the options.

The agent asked for his e-mail so he could send him the information. He did not have an e-mail.

The agent was very surprised and stated that even though he did not have an e-mail he built an empire, imagine if he had one where would he be today?

The business executive reflected and said: I would be a plumber at Microsoft! The moral of the story is:

The internet is not the solution for your life.

If you work hard, even if you do not have a computer, you can become a millionaire

If you received this message via e-mail your chances are you will become a plumber not a millionaire!

Have a great day.....

We do not have to go far; the television give us examples of people's attitudes like finding personal values and returning them or dedicating themselves to noble causes.

What should be normal attitude to have, becomes big news.

We long for the progress in the moral aspect, but we are hindered by an opposite force that prevents good deeds from happening: it takes special people to overcome these barriers.

Today, with the distortion of values, many put aside the moral standards to achieve goals, using selfish reasons like pride, vanity and lack of common sense to rule their life.

In a corporate context, the workforce fails to complete projects do not arrive at solutions for them due to these poor attitudes. It causes business losses and affects the end result.

The biggest loser is the group: how many projects or problems could be solved, if the attitudes were correct?

Amazing how personal misconduct can affect a business!

Not to be forgotten are the environment and safety in life and at work.

Only with consistent effort one can change the Planet for the better.

Negligence or lack of responsible attitudes generates great losses for health, balance and social well being.

Necessity causes man to develop new endeavor in all fields. The proof is on the technological advances that create products and cyclic processes: we extract from nature, there is a transformation, production and direct or indirect return to nature. It is wisdom in action.

Few people have noticed that there is a need to save in life, not only by the monetary return, but the need to manage the best way possible, thus respecting future generations.

The preservation of physical integrity also is attitude of a higher conscience: big losses are incurred for each accident that happens.

The suffering is shared not only by the person, but family, company, society, nation.

The independence of the human being relays mostly on his physical and mental sanity! It starts in the "Conscience"!

Attitude

Attitude to change
From the wrong to the right
For the one that fools himself
Trading surety for uncertainty

Sergio A. Meneghetti

CHAPTER VIII

The Hiring process

We have described at length the predominant characteristics that a future professional must have.

The future is near but on the Earth, all are human beings and still mostly imperfect.

We carry a load of fallacies; the weight of this burden will always be proportionally opposite to someone with virtuous shoulder.

If we, as humans have to evolve and this process is slow (we only solidify learning passing many tests along existence) we must have the responsibility to take the first step urgently. It is not just a matter of self improvement, but of basic principles to be applied in order to be hired, therefore improving the quality of life: in a more blunt way, our survival in this world. Observing facts, we notice that many people are growing materially, devoid of honesty, acting under false pretenses but at the end the future will charge the soul. There is no illusion, the payback is happening now and time will make sure it "collects from all" that are not in sync with the world.

This false freedom that the world is experiencing is for each of us to show our true face true character. Whoever has good or bad traits will be tested.

Dear reader: On this Earth, nobody "owns the truth", but for sure, life is pure math. Whoever generates credit will have credit, and if debt is created it will have to be paid.

Note:

In more than thirty years of work, we have observed several situations:

People with power within the company that get disconnected from the rest and end up needing their lowest class subordinates.

Arrogant people that lost their position.
People that started from the bottom up and distinguished themselves.
People that barely did their work and lost their job.
Daring people that grew significantly.
Good Natured and compassionate people.
Deceiving people and traitors.

They all received according to their merit.

Important to keep in mind.

"Man is not the position he occupies in a Company or government institution, he is in that position for a period of time"
This book is dedicated to the new professionals, they are easier to train. Whoever is ahead of them will have a hard time with the change.
To assimilate something new is easier than braking old habits and beliefs.

There is a new philosophy brewing. It has already been perceived by competent professionals: the values that truly matter.
When going on an interview think about this:

Sincerity, modesty, to be yourself, to channel all you internal potential with faith. This internal confidence produces good results, especially because enhances your self esteem.
It is normal for people to portray something beyond their reality, trying to impress and convince the interviewer.
They do not realize that the interviewer has a lot more experience and psychology.
Nowadays, those who select candidates search for the inner essence and are more desirable to have inexperience with modesty than to be experienced with arrogance.

I have interviewed candidates in the past and the decisive factor was how the person came across. The professional curriculum or academic took second place.

In the selection all hired became very good professionals.

"Have the moral courage to be "you"!

Good training is important, but not everybody had the means to attend the best Universities and that is why it is unfair to discriminate against them.

If you work in the Human Resources area, be considerate with the people to be hired.

Remember that the best doctor, philosopher, psychologist, life manager did not attend the best schools of his time.

Hiring

Selective process
That carves the stone
Values the heart
In love and labor

Sergio Meneghetti-2007

CHAPTER IX

Coexistence

To coexist is not only a matter of personal experiences, but it is cultivating the ability to accept situations whether they are good or bad. To be near pain or happiness, building balanced relationships or skidding on ignorance and meanness.

We spend a lot of time co-existing with people in our workplace. It is similar to a marriage because they have a common goal: looking for successful, lasting results.

It is a privilege to work in a pleasant environment, enjoying what one does for a living. It is priceless! It is counterproductive to have people that in certain instances disrupt the harmony at work.

An apprehensive worker is unbalanced and is bound to have health and emotional unbalance.

Work has to bring not only sustenance, but also enjoyment.

The presence of problematic people ends up killing the group motivation and generates losses for the company, no matter how good the professional is.

It was discussed on TV the negative effects that annoying people provoke at work.

This condition was diagnosed as a disease and has to be treated.

The opposite holds true: it is a pleasure to work with balanced, calm people: only benefits the group and the company.

A healthy environment is the most important requirement for a business to be successful.

It is total concentration of positive energy towards the same purpose.

Another type of co-existence has to do with insecurity.

It can be worse than the personal co-existence because it places people's lives at risk.

The losses are immeasurable because it affects family, friends and even the environment. At the end everybody loses.

How many disasters have happened! The cause could the result of co-existence with danger. It is a blind trust believing that nothing can happen.

To protect health and the environment is everybody's duty.

Never wait to take the initiative, be the first!

To know how to co-exist means prolonging life!

To co-exist with: despair, idleness, boredom, unnecessary suffering, spite, lack of will and perspective, negative and discouraging conditions, generates a slow pacing working atmosphere.

A positive coexistence that is creative, dynamic and concise, progressive and present guarantees excellent results.

On the personal co-existence level, nobody is reference of behavior the way we believe. Everything around us has to be taking in consideration in order to attain the balance and acceptance of general behavior.

In general, the good environment is a give and take, where we surrender to the side in need and vice-versa. .

Co-existence

Above the art of living
There is a whole science
Wisdom to co-exist and evolve
And expand ones' conscience!

Sergio A. Meneghetti

CHAPTER X

Cerebral Dominance

Life is an eternal school, and we must be able to learn the most we can. . . Years ago, we attended a training seminar in which we were given a very interesting test called Cerebral Dominance. This test consisted of 128 questions (ready-made phrases) and the theme was about personal preferences and how we would make our decisions. . . There was a chart divided in 4 parts. With answers in feedback, it showed the results of your personal tendencies and characteristics.

Below a summarized description of the 4 groups of cerebral preferences or expressions of thought:

SE= Superior Left- The Analytical
One that analyzes, quantifies, is logical, critical, and realistic, likes numbers, understands economic affairs, and knows how things work.

IE= Inferior Left- The controller
One that takes preventive measures, establishes procedures, is a doer, is trustworthy, organized, neat, punctual and a planner.

ID= Inferior Right- The communicator

One that is compassionate, likes to teach, affects people, communicates emotional, talks a lot and is sensitive.

SD= Superior Right- the Tester
One that is creative, speculates, dares, is impulsive, breaks the rules, likes surprises, curious and jokes around. . .

The result was very interesting: each individual has one characteristic in different areas: meaning that, if someone has difficulties in certain areas, does not mean lack of capacity, but only that he has not learned or have natural aptitude for it.

In my case, I am the superior right (SD) that corresponds to creativity, marketing, intuition, composition. However I am not into numbers, economics, accounting, etc. . . .

The results demonstrate that human beings are very complex in the mental capacity and we all have something to offer to the opposites and vice versa.

How far does our exploration can reach, emotionally and spiritually?

So little is invested in our mind which is priceless, considering that millions are spent in the development of material things and leisure.

However, we are beginning the "Era of the Mind" and we are already having a positive and practical approach otherwise would be a waste of time and effort.

I believe that we came to Earth to make it a better place!

The sooner we utilize the mental concept, more energy will be saved in the progress development and will be economical and ecologically correct.

When we use this emotional intelligence (cerebral dominance) we contribute more as a whole by using our aptitudes.

That is why I try to channel my energy so I can get higher productivity in my endeavors, be it at work or personally.

Since human beings only use a fraction of this mental capacity, it is amazing how much each individual can give in benefit of mankind.

We bombard our minds with information, so we are capable to do our work, to study, have a personal and social life.

Observing the special people that contribute to the moral, artistic, spiritual and scientific advances, we will find that they all use the most precious information which originated from an internal source.

The Mind is very powerful. The I am is the mind or our conscience, therefore the power resides in the I!

The mind is the machine; the conscience is the commander of this machine.

Therefore, a group of people will find it easier to understand the intuitive phenomena.

Another group will have difficulty because has analytic abilities.

Mind

Mind that speaks
Mind that remains silent
Mind that sees
Mind that feels

Mind only
Mind seed
Opaque mind
Transparent mind

Mind that teaches
Mind that learns
Mind that fascinates
Mind present.

True mind
Mind that lies
Interesting mind
Happy mind.

Mind in the past
Mind in the present
Tired mind
Ardent mind.

Open mind
Negligent mind
Mind that alerts
Careless mind.

Mind essence of being
Intelligent mind
Mind that is itself
Mind that is never absent.

Sergio A. Meneghetti

CHAPTER XI

Dimensions: the Relative and the Absolute

To have a better understanding of Intuition, I will give a personal opinion about this matter that is discussed at length in the wonderful work of Professor Pietro Ubaldi: the Great Synthesis. For many it is difficult to grasp the concepts of the controversial subject. It would be ideal to read the TRILOGY:

1. Great messages-is composed of seven messages received through Intuition and the Author's Biography.
2. The Great Synthesis- a summary of spiritual and scientific solutions elaborated by the intuitive process.
3. The Noures- author's explanation about the techniques and reception of the trends of thought.

The reader will be able to envision through the book collection above how much Intuition can help reach higher levels in science and spirituality.

First of all, it is important to assimilate difficult concepts for the current thinking: time and space, absolute and relative.

Space is a dimensional phase in which something is located and this space includes three dimensions: linear, surface and volume. According to the Great Synthesis, the degradation of the atomic matter gives birth to a new trinity, the time birth (fourth dimension.).

The second phase is consciousness (fifth dimension and current stage of humanity).

Finally the third phase, the super consciousness sixth dimension, where humanity enters the absolute and the only way to enter it is through moral evolution.

Adding time and space we obtain the Relative where everything "was, is and will be somewhere". Using scientific methods one can situate something some time and in some point in space.

But is it possible that existence would be limited to this "relative"?

If this were be the case how do we explain the prophesies made by famous people in history?

How could they go through matter and "see" something that had not happened yet?

And why theses visions always are so important historically as to justify such personal phenomenon?

Reason loses its power when we try to answer these questions. At this point, the learning through intuition begins, and we can have a better concept of the absolute.

Absolute, according to reason is hard to understand because it involves the Relative and in this phase there is no time or space as human beings are aware. In the absolute, all "is" nothing was or nothing will be.

Commonly speaking, we can obtain the answers to explain the Phenomenology used by the prophets. It also applies to certain people that in a major scale are able to foresee situations that will happen in the future through daily moments, meditation or dreams.

These individuals through need or personal evolution penetrate in the absolute and only the "new" man can "see" the Absolute, meaning the man that after effort and struggle evolved to the point of being able to absorb such concepts.

Life progresses from the infinitesimal to the greatest. This phenomenon is present regardless of Influence of the surroundings or creeds. Because life is cyclical soon after birth, the death process begins to close the cycle. In the meantime development happens and so on.

Based on that premise, we cannot picture man in only one point in history. He participates many times, so he can evolve helping the environment and the planet as a whole. Thus, man is an eternal expansion of consciousness and more and more understands what exists beyond the tangible, reaching the senses.

There is a lot of talk about the sixth sense, but it is a mystery for other religious beliefs and for part of the population does not mean anything and it does not attract their attention.

There is a great amount of information about this subject (intuition, inspiration or feeling).

There're no miracles, the fact many phenomenon cannot be proved scientifically, due to the stage science is now.

It is vital for mankind to deepen the knowledge in this subject, pairing science and technology arriving to a common denominator. If there is such a law that rules over tangible things or measurable in the Universe, this law also has to rule over things that are moral and sensorial. As described in the Pierto Ubaldi's Great Synthesis, there are physical effects and moral causes as are also moral effects and physical causes. They don't exist isolated from each other: this leaves many unanswered questions in science. Its consciousness will cause man to great Life advances in science and ethics.

When man retracts from these facts: science and faith, he will be ignoring important factors preventing advancement and breaking the link between them, thus leaving many questions without answers.

To summarize, man must leave superstition and cold reason aside to advance.

The mind must assimilate new ideas, opening the way for the senses to be materialized.

By avoiding the existing religious and scientific facts, it is unconceivable to believe only one existence on this Earth because it defies reason. . . if God created all things (nothing creates nothing) and if we were created by chance it would never be so perfectly organized as it is, the same applies to life as we know it. From the mineral through the human form there is great wisdom. Therefore God could not possibly make such a complex creature such as man for only one lifetime.

Because everybody has God as a symbol of perfection and justice, it would be unfair to create beings with distinct capacities and abilities. This fact escapes logic. It is not necessary to accept this theory, let's take in consideration the following concepts:

Man is the pure creation of a Supreme Being.

Man evolves from mineral to vegetable to animal and finally to human and to a higher scale to a genius or saint.

It is possible to have several passages through this life as humans and in these phases man acquires knowledge and has experiences creating situations that generate other future aspects positive or negative.

If this supposed evolution is possible, then man has to follow a rising path, has to struggle and work, suffer and love, embrace all life trials, accumulate experiences and lifetimes solidifying knowledge.

Only this way he can be sure of what he says, feels, teaches and will have the humbleness to learn more.

Man of little faith gets delayed in this evolution because they assume having the whole truth, but only have a faint idea of the truth.

They are misled and self aggrandized, not being aware of the fragile foundations in which they based all their advances and science.

The only way man advances is to carry within himself faith and science, both generating great strength, moral and scientific that promote advances for the future.

The genius extract raw materials of his findings from himself, he has the power to be inspired by forces beyond the material realm, prodding ethereal areas without his body having consciousness of the phenomenon.

He detects this feeling in its essence. The power comes from his mind, in the eagerness to receive the unknown, "something" that words cannot express.

The genius or saint starts already utilizing the super conscience or the Sixth Dimension (third phase of the second trinity), transport themselves where no machine can, they dive into the Absolute and from there receive all the necessary information.

There is no need for labs or writings.

Superior forces guide them and show the path they must take and what to look for.

The genius foresees and promotes advances therefore he must have ethics and a baggage of solid knowledge so he can understand and absorb the new discoveries and make good use of it.

Many intellectual people above average are spread throughout the world where they are needed and this scientific intuitive advancement will guide science in the future, as well as institutions and corporations.

Through renouncement, kindness and learning, man will share the hidden treasure that is dormant in his heart.

Absolute and Relative

When we understand the Relative
We penetrate into the Absolute.
Relationships shape the Relative
And the union molds the Absolute.

Sergio A. Meneghetti

CHAPTER XII

Intuitive Experiences

Obs: This is the most difficult part of this book, as we will have to divulge our most private thoughts to be able to attest to the subject discussed.

The purpose in writing this book is to relate to the reader facts based on my life experience. It was not learned in any school, even though literature gave me a better understanding, in the pursuit of personal development.

I try to use it in all areas of life, including my work and it has helped me a great deal.

"Intuition is not achieved in school; you are born with it and must strive to develop it." This phenomenon has followed me since childhood with great benefits.

I am a common person, with virtues but still have many liabilities to overcome.

Nothing comes to me easily, all is achieved with great effort and must try not to give up or let less noble thoughts take control and interfere with this hard ascent to self improvement. I thank God for granting me this precious gift called Intuition and for all the information I had access to as far as personal development, knowledge and experiences.

I will deal with Intuition, the way it manifests from my personal point of view. Each person has a specific way to sense or perceive it: I hope that my experiences will enable people to identify with their feelings, thus using it as a tool for personal and spiritual improvement. As explained before describing the intuitive process, I am a receiver unit and have to be in tune with the emitting source. To be in sync with something subtle and in a higher level we must be ingenious, give up many worldly habits.

Habits such: eating red meat, pork, drinking, depressing news, low moral level programs or movies, aggressive words and name-calling, sleazy environments, etc, .

All above are like static makers and end up interfering with the positive intuitive reception. Why avoid red meat?

It slows down much of digestive process and sometimes causes drowsiness. It is observed that several people from different religious backgrounds when need to meditate, they fast. The reason is to maintain body and mind lighter and more serene.

Why avoid drinking?

Drinking affects the nervous system creating body imbalance and loss of normalcy.

Why avoid depressing information?

Bad news also hinders the positive thoughts from flowing.

A mind that thrives on negative thoughts cannot generate positive ones.

The mind will be too preoccupied with these news and there will be no room for a more subliminal reception.

Why avoid movies or programs of low level morals?

It is important to elevate thoughts and leave the mind free of less noble things.

Why avoid aggressive words and name-calling?

When man has this attitude, obviously he is unbalanced which is directly opposite to mental elevation and personal improvement.

Why avoid low immoral environments?

You attract good things in a good environment.

Obs: We must take in consideration that human beings make choices and must be respected, nevertheless.

Naturally the reader may argue that it is a lot to give up, however everything has a price.

Habits should not interfere with the intuition development.

Every person already has intuition ingrained in their soul, in different levels, some not even aware they possess it.

People should learn how to know themselves well so they can observe and distinguish intuition from reason.

I have my own particular method to perceive and many can have similar characteristics.

It is hard to define a feeling or internal perception, usually we use comparisons. Otherwise it becomes difficult to explain.

I will relay some events in which my intuition played a key role, describing the way it was perceived:

Case 1

I worked with a company for six years, working seven days in each shift. from 8AM-4PM 4PM–12AM – 12AM-8AM.

On the 24th of July, 1982 I was on the 4PM-12AM shift. About 2 PM while I was having lunch at home suddenly a pressing thought came to my mind, like the sound of someone whispering in my ear: Fire in the manufacturing plant!

This thought was followed by a flashing light. I got apprehensive and anxious but went to work as usual.

At 5PM that day I heard a small pop, checked the external area surrounding the lab, across from the production processing site and noticed a side filter leak. This leak would spew a steady product flow, but of no consequence.

This minor incident gave me some relief because I thought that was what had sensed earlier in the day. However, by 6PM I heard another pop followed by a steady noise, checked again around the lab and noticed a fast growing fire on the left wing of the building. That confirmed the intuition I had at lunch. The fire lasted for 2 hours and fortunately there were no fatalities.

Even though it can be classified as premonition, the velocity and characteristics of the event I would classify it as an "Internal Manifestation".

There is no control for this type of intuitive happening. It does not depend on our will, but we can channel the reception.

Case 2

My wife had a 1990 auto that she used to go to work.

We placed an ad for sale through several channels. I met a car dealer who offered to sell the car at his dealership and keep a percentage of the sale. At the same time, another store owner contacted by me called and asked to have the car appraised because he had a buyer.

I took the car from the lot, drove it to the store owner but the deal did not go through. I kept the car for a week, talked to the dealer again and he agreed to have the car returned to the lot to be sold. On the way to the dealer, "intuition" told me that the dealer was going to buy the car from me.

When I got there, the dealer told me: I will buy your car! I depend on credit approval for one of my clients and upon confirmation, we close the deal.

However, the client was never approved and my car could not be bought.

It was odd because the feeling was so strong about the sale. . . . . .

Two months went by and finally intuition paid off. The dealer did buy the car.

This phenomenon I call External Manifestation due to someone "telling" my mind what would happen and materialized.

Again, this type of phenomenon that does not depend on reason and it pays off to be prepared like a tuned receptor ready to capture the message sent.

Case 3

For information purposes, I worked in the plastics development area, and the multinationals were the best clients.

Throughout 2000, the company had some ongoing projects to supply 3 new materials needed by a Japanese manufacturer. In order to facilitate the project it was decided that they would import the raw material and formulas from a group located in Japan.

With the formulas and raw material, we started production in our laboratory.

After the samples were made, a process of characterization started in order to verify the quality of the products and if it corresponded to the client's requirements and specifications.

These products had been manufactured in Japan successfully in the past, by using the same raw materials. Again new products were manufactured but to no avail.

It was concluded that the products in Brazil did not meet the requirements needed and were rejected.

We would have to send the products to Japan to be tested.

New products were manufactured but to no avail. The question was: should we send the samples as they were or not?

Due to the fact that there was a deadline to meet, the samples were sent back as they were.

On Friday I asked my boss if I could try to make the samples on Saturday.

He agreed, but was not confident that the experiments would be successful after so many trials had been made. I had a "feeling" that I could do it, but did not know how.

I started to analyze the work done before and I had to come up with a new technique. I started to pray for help the solution started ton take shape in my mind, showing me what to do. I needed to make a rational verification of intuition and put the idea to work.

The process began. I manufactured the materials and prepared them for tests to be conducted on Monday. On the first phase of room temperature testing, I noticed great improvement. Then I tested in low temperature. The testing would resume at 2PM. Just before 2PM, my boss stopped at the lab and asked me if I had worked on Saturday and after I confirmed he ask me if I had any tests ready. Even though I was successful at first, I told him I did not. I wanted to complete all testing before I let him know about the results. My boss appreciated my efforts but informed me and my friend that it was bound to be a failure.

I did not say anything, but we both knew that, based from the success of the first phase, The results of next phase would be positive. We concluded the testing and sure enough, all ended up well.

Next day I was congratulated by management. Also I must give them credit to them for letting us exercise our autonomy. Without it several projects would not have come to a happy ending.

To summarize this case: the samples we made again and sent to Japan. The results were better then expected.

After this testing phase, there was a commercial dilemma to be resolved; production costs came very close to the cost of the imported materials. The reason; import duties. A meeting was scheduled with the client and it was suggested that a domestic version would be made to meet the minimum requirements of specifications, but less costly with mainly domestic duties imposed.

Based on the latest technology process obtained through the intuitive process, the team started to develop new product versions and in a short period of time obtained products with better characteristics that met the demands of the client.

Result: We reached our objective and started selling products.

These products called the attention of the auto industry, thus attracting new clients.

Another important aspect was to transfer this latest technology to all products with similar characteristics, achieving the utilization reduction of imported raw material.

What, at first was the need to complete a project, became a financial principle, giving the company's products competitive costs generating millions in profits. With this new technology the materials became more ecologically correct because better properties generate less weight, thus less fuel consumption and causes less pollution.

In this case, intuition was beneficial beyond any expectation, shortened research and testing, saved money, time, labor, raw materials, avoided formation of residues from testing and opened a new technological path.

This achievement could be attained by anybody using Intuition as a Working tool. I take the credit in this case for knowing how to use this tool at the right time aided by a capable team.

Imagine the potential every professional can develop in his area of expertise, as well as in the personal and artistic field.

The Universe has at our disposition an inexhaustible source of precious information: it is up to us open this divine door and channel the best for the common good.

This is the so called Driven Manifestation, meaning the utilization of intuition wisely to obtain high minded results, even if only small ones.

We must always be attentive to our thoughts, as the mind can be receptive to information of an important function or outcome.

Case 4-

I have a friend, head of a multinational that worked overseas. Due to the busy lives we both had, we had little contact, sometimes exchanging e-mails.

At that time, one day I felt the need to contact him. My intuition "told" me that it was something concerning the diversification of his business. Since he was a very capable businessman, at first I hesitated to contact him. But I could not get him out of my mind. When I relayed my feelings about the subject, to my surprise, immediately he sent me a message that read:

Thank you for the information and references. We are at present time conducting a detailed study about this topic also in Brazil. We should have the results by the second semester of 2007 to make a decision. I am thankful for your input.

Never before had I had any contact regarding this confidential matter.

The question is:

Why the intuition was so strong to the point of bothering me so much?

How would this matter come to my mind, if it was already being in progress overseas?

In my humble opinion, it was a warning or a positive reinforcement to the subject at hand. It is a matter of time when we will see the results, that I hope will the best possible.

For ethical reasons, it is not be possible to discuss things related to the business any further.

Note:

This is the second edition of this book written by me. At the time, LyondellBasell Industries was founded on 21st of December, 2007, the third largest Chemical Corporation in the world. Mr. Volker Trautz is the CEO, the author of the e-mail mentioned earlier.

Case 5

During 1996, I participated in a project called "Multi Skill" The goal was to multiply knowledge in other areas of the company. I left temporarily the lab and worked for a while training on the petrochemical process.

There was a special maneuver in loading and unloading the carts full of propylene gas to a reservoir. During this process, that required maximum security, there were two lock valves, one manual, the other automatic, apart from each other about 40 cm.

At the end there was steel over sleeve, plastic coated, with diameter of more or less 2 inches, which would be connected to the cart.

As a matter of security everything was tested to prevent accidents, I then proceeded to open the automatic valve to verify if there was gas between them. The gas pressure was eight atmospheres. When I was going to open the valve, "something" told me to get away from it. Following my instinct, I distanced myself from the valve and turned the button.

The over sleeve supported on a pedestal, suddenly acted as strong fast whip, spewing gas on my face. The impact of the ending was so intense that it broke a chunk of cement from the ground.

Had I not listened to my intuition I would be dead by now!

Case 6

At the beginning of 2010, I was anxious to close a deal on one of my properties Selling it would prevent me from losing this one and another one which I owned.

The one to be sold had a mortgage and the proceeds would be used to finish the construction of my house and pay for the expenses. It was urgent!

An offer was made, but it was not acceptable, I tried different ways to solve the problem but without success. My wife suggested that I use my Intuition, after all I wrote a book about it!

That is exactly what I decided to do. During that week I concentrated on my emotional and spiritual equilibrium and treated the situation as follows:

I "saw" myself closing the deal, but 30% lower that the asking price.
I "saw" myself not accepting the deal and waiting for a better offer.

The right decision would be the one that made me feel at ease, I took the second option, decided to wait at the risk of losing everything!

I declined the first offer which was the right thing to do, as another came that met my needs.

Had I not listened to Intuition, reason would have taken over and the result: a bad business decision.

Case 7

After Haiti was struck by a devastating Hurricane, January 12, 2010, I wrote an article that had a good review.

While I was at work, I felt the urge to send the article abroad. The idea kept pounding on my head nonstop. Before the computer, I used Google to translate the contents of my article and sent it to the State

Department of the United States. The automatic reply acknowledged the receipt and thanked me for sending it.

I recall seeing the Obama Blog, decided to look for the White House site and found the connection to the president. I filled all the requirements and sent the article. The site replied that the article was too long and needed to be edited.

After the second request to shorten the article, I finally received a positive reply.

On Easter weekend with relatives visiting us for the occasion, I mentioned to my older sister about the article sent to Obama and that I had not been contacted yet, and thought they might be giving some consideration to what I wrote. The same afternoon, my brother in law asked me to use the computer to retrieve his messages. While he was doing it, I asked him to check my messages. To my surprise there was a Thank you message from Obama thanking me for the article. (See attached message).

Segue:
Thank you for your message

De: The White House - Presidential Correspondence (noreply-WHPC@whitehouse. gov)
!Você pode não conhecer este remetente. Marcar como conflável?Marcar como lixo
Enviada: sexta-feira, 2 de abril de 2010 18:13:36
Para: sergio. xxxxxxxx@hotmail. com
Dear Friend:

Thank you for writing regarding the situation in Haiti. The earthquake that struck Haiti on January 12 shocked the world. The loss of life is heartbreaking, and the suffering and destruction are devastating. The images of this tragedy remind us of our common humanity and have invoked our Nation's enduring spirit of generosity and compassion.

My Administration has responded with a swift, coordinated, and aggressive relief effort, among the largest in our history. I designated Dr. Rajiv Shah, Administrator of the United States Agency for International Development, as our Government's unified disaster coordinator. He is leading America's effort alongside the United Nations, together with international aid and nongovernmental organizations on the ground in Haiti. I have also enlisted the help of Presidents Bush and Clinton, who have launched a major fundraising effort for Haiti, and those who wish to help should visit: ClintonBushHaitiFund. org.

With a pledge of our full support, I assured Haitian President René Préval that America stands by the Haitian people. We must meet their needs through sustained assistance to help Haiti recover and rebuild. Bringing relief to the millions who are suffering poses tremendous challenges--navigating crumbled roads and damaged ports, and finding shelter for the homeless--but we must forge ahead to help restore the Haitian people's energy and optimism for a more hopeful future.

We are fortunate that our Nation has a unique capacity to reach out swiftly and broadly, and Americans have always come together to serve others in times of great need. The dedication of our military personnel and rescue teams, and the goodwill of millions of Americans lending a helping hand, demonstrate the courage and decency of our people.

To learn more about our efforts, visit:
www. WhiteHouse. gov/HaitiEarthquake. We will stand with the people of Haiti and keep them in our thoughts and prayers.

Sincerely,
Barack Obama

To be a part of our agenda for change, join us at www. WhiteHouse. gov

Below the message sent to Obama:

Haiti's Rebirth

"It is from old seeds that one builds his new garden!" Haiti, a land branded in the beginning by slavery By the past, less distant by war and desecration Today stricken by Nature with its destruction strength Tomorrow, it will rebirth with love and construction

Man goes through several phases in this life: they are necessary for his achievements, freedom and maturity. It is the eternal trajectory.
The rock shifting deep in the Earth, natural action of nature comes to level down all people from a region.

Now rich and poor, ignorants and wisemen, leaders and followers, right and left wing politicians, old and young, religious and atheists, black and whites, snobs and meek, idle and workers, victims and executioners, bosses and employees, givers and takers, every duality loses what is ephemeral, only the result of each individual's work remains.

While the world pans the victims and solidarity, charity and compassion are in evidence, the ones that remain have the responsibility to rebuild the nation solid in its foundation with PEACE without discrimination.

Be that the older brothers from this world share their kindness, helping financially and with knowledge.
Be that aid relief which will transform this suffering place into a new haven where prosperity is dynamic and productive.
Teach this country to extract growth from their work: charity is welcome, but soon dries out and gets lost in time.
To the people, be that they bury the negative past with the dead, maintaining their qualities and new perspective for a better future.

Be that they remember the good and charitable souls that lost their lives in the Haitian soil. They were many and deserve all the gratitude.

The suffering is felt, showing mankind's fragility and what is important in this life. It comes silently, sometimes calm or furious with full strength, even though is bad, it can also be a blessing that wake us up from the illusions, leading us to the right path: (we only lack the understanding).

Suffering destroys the love feelings and the solidarity in someone's heart, stirs emotions, then the world calms down and aches for healing, it is the opposite of violence that creates friction and vengeance.

History has shown that many countries that were ravaged by disaster or war rebuilt themselves and became better than before (thanks to the people's good will and effort).

Haiti is the room of the moment in this great house that demands attention and refurbishment, not forgetting that there other Haitis that also need to be taking care of.

Each cent that is invested in the progress of our needy brothers will reap the best returns in the future. . .

What is the greatest desire in life? The pursuit of Happiness!

So let everybody do their share to attain this goal!

We are thankful to all the heroes of this endeavor that have helped, are helping and will help to rebuild Haiti!

Sergio A Meneghetti
1/18/2010

Note: Between sending the article and the White House reply, something odd happen: In my mind I "saw" several times an enormous hand holding a small sheet of paper by the tips of the thumb and the index finger.

What are the odds of a normal person from the interior of Brazil, not famous, nor being part to the government, to send a message (using

Google translator) to the President of the wealthiest nation on Earth and receive a personal reply?

I think it is easier to win the lottery!

That proves again the power of Intuition. The impossible became reality.

Case 8

On the evening of my birthday on 4/12/1999, I dreamed with four men inviting me to join their small company. They were very sad. The next morning things happened exactly as in the dream, but my intuition came to me as a warning.

I decided to accept the invitation, however it only caused me problems and financial losses. That explained the sadness I saw in the dream!

The only good thing I got from it was the experience I gained as a partner and that was when I wrote my first poem called "The Writing". It opened the doors to what I do today. There is an old saying: suffering is the spring that motivates us to personal improvement. We can always learn from our experiences.

In this case it came through a dream.

Note: Curiosities with the number 12

On the

4/12/1994 I got a car from a consortium.

4/12/1998 I retired after 30 years of work.

12/12/2012 I wrote a farewell poem for the company where I worked.

12/12/2013 The Company released me (after many requests on my part)

09/12/2014 I have just finished my book in English.

On my humble opinion; The Universe conspires in our favor or according to what we deserve.

I documented the benefits of Intuition, some disastrous because I ignored the warnings and in other instances they were beneficial and all ended well.

I feel that the above cases are good examples and would be a waste of time to relay more experiences. After all my intention was to synthesize the contents as much as I could.

I will try to explain my feelings referent to this phenomenon, enabling the reader to see the difference between own thoughts and intuition.

The first thing to keep in mind: with the exception of Driven Manifestation, intuition is not controlled by the receptor; it does not depend on will. We cannot say: I am going to intuit now! All depends of the emitting source.

We must be prepared, with a refined sense so we intercept what comes to us.

When I was a teenager, I had to ride the bus and played a game trying to guess which bus line would come next. Most of the time I would get it right Unfortunately I was not at the bus stop at the same time every day, otherwise with practice I could memorize the bus schedule. Even then I started noticing this means of communication but never got into it. I would let my mind free, would try to control my thoughts. But reason is intuition inhibitor. It is vital to have the mind free.

I would let it happen and with time I started paying more attention to the phenomenon. By 1988 I came across the Pierto Ubaldi's the Great Synthesis. It was like a treasure reading the book, I found out that it had been written through the intuitive process. Later on I read two more books, Great Messages and The Noures: this one was an explanation of how the Great Synthesis was created, how the phenomenon would manifest and what Ubaldi had to do was to make it flow.

That is when I started to pay close attention to my inner self to become a good reception tool and get credit for it.

I stopped eating red meat and pork because they are difficult to digest and interfere with intuition. I avoided name calling, drinking, anything immoral, violent news, terror movies, bad environments, reasons already stated before.

There is no imposition on my part; everybody has free will to choose the path to follow. What I am trying to do is to show the way. Everyone experiences sensations in specific ways, but I feel they will be similar to mine.

When I get apprehensive with something different in my mind that means that I will have to deal with it later.

When I also feel uneasy, it can mean something unpleasant. To illustrate this feeling, in 1999 going to work at night, and I had been very uncomfortable all day. The answer: I was stalked and robbed that night.

In this case we ask for God's protection so worse things are prevented from happening. Prayer is also very powerful and can avoid or minimize tragedies.

Intuition also produces positive results. For instance I enrolled in a literary contest and had two poems that were selected from thirteen hundred that entered the contest. I was selected for the first phase and competed with 640 more poems.

Many times I tried to channel positive thoughts but due to the interference of the daily matters I had to take care of, things happened and there was nothing I could about it.

These perceptions do not apply only for big events; they also work for minor daily routine and at work

The main thing is to detect details of the inner sensibility, to our best productive benefit.

Regarding the Driven Manifestation, below the guidelines to follow: Examine the subject and confirm if it is a noble cause.

Seek a serene place where you can pray, preferably in a wholesome environment

Ask for divine guidance on solving problems and how to reach your goals if it is creative, new or unknown.

Free your mind: reason will interfere even though you are focused on your objective. You will be wasting unnecessary energy and blocking your mind.

You can utilize meditation also. It expands the mental, helping the relaxation and freeing of the mind.

Usually these suggestions are followed also for religious means, emotional well being, health or inner development. Work helps humanity to evolve; therefore it also has a divine characteristic and deserves this type of attention.

If Intuition is used as a new method of work and research, humanity will be speeding the evolution of Earth and humanity a lot faster.

There is an economy in life that must be observed, because it will be the result of inner growth. This growth will make the processes simpler, pure, clean and optimized.

It is the cycle of basic to perfection.

Manual labor exerted less effort when replaced by animals, development of tools, machinery, and information, electronic controls, now evolving to the intuitive or mental. This intuitive potential can and must be used by everybody in all areas, starting with the least sophisticated worker up to the highest position in command.

I believe that what we can achieve is far more reaching than we can imagine and hope this book can be the motivation for people to develop and open this path wider.

Dear Reader! I am aware that my work is still in the early stages, but that is the way things start.

The success of each goal starts from inertia. Results will happen only by turning the wheel!

SUCCESS

Be that my hands,
Operate the progress
And that intuition in the mind
Be the beginning of success.

Sergio Antonio Meneghetti

CHAPTER XIII

Afterword

In preceding chapters, the author tried to cover matters related to moral, spiritual qualities and complex issues like time, relative, absolute, space and intuition.

They may seem not to be related but within the Universe, all is connected somehow and we belong to it as a whole.

We cannot escape from this setting since it is a system with hermetic characteristics. Therefore, we must learn how to coexist the best we can.

Following this trend of thought, it begins small and imperfect and through evolution becomes perfect in the material and spiritual realm.

The free will is proportional to the moral evolution as opposed to determinism. . We will have more free will over the things we are aware of or are responsible for. The lack of knowledge will restrict the field of action and will be subjected to solutions beyond our control. We must develop a good foundation: intellectual, emotional, social and spiritual stimulating the evolution process." Good intuition is linked to the evolution of the individual."

In the professional workplace if one wants to get a good job, he must not only be prepared academically, but also morally, spiritually and emotionally.

Eventually this will be the standard rule for the job selection. Hidden talents we all possess, but rarely use it to progress: they will be the decisive factor in landing a higher position in a company.

When an individual enters the job market, he must shed all the negative feelings like vanity, pride, and envy and strive to apply the intuitive aptitudes with persistence to achieve success.

How to develop this intuitive aptitude?

By becoming aware of its existence and the first step is self improvement.

It can develop in the following instances:

Be consciously aware of its presence.

Perceiving and feeling it.

Detecting and separating it from normal thoughts.

Believing in it, but also being able to see it logically.

Being balanced mentally and spiritually, so it becomes easier to channel and understand it.

To know yourself and to be able to distinguish the external from the internal Corporations in the future will select employees with high moral standards and because of that criteria, they will be more efficient and generate more profit.

With a selected group working with the principles of intuition and spirituality, corporations will be able to stay in business longer and will have the opportunity to expand their horizons.

The reverse holds true: the unqualified worker will not be able to occupy higher positions and will hold only menial jobs.

We are responsible for the betterment of society, by doing the best we can and progress, no matter the size or extension of our action. The world is after all, the sum of small actions.

Conclusion

I can only hope
That this conclusion
Be crystalline like water
And solid as the ground is.

Sergio Antonio Meneghetti